Unreported Truth: Technocracy 2030- 2050

Vaccine Frauds, Cyber Attacks, World Wars &
Population Control; Exposed!

Rebel Press Media

Dislcaimer

1

Our other books

Check out our other books for other unreported news, exposed facts and debunked truths, and more.

Join the exclusive Rebel Press Media Circle!

You will get a new updates about the unreported reality delivered in your inbox every Friday.

Sign up here today:

https://campsite.bio/rebelpressmedia

Introduction

What independent scientists were already warning about has now been confirmed: vaccinated people become much more susceptible to some corona mutations. A study by Tel Aviv University shows that people who have been injected with the Pfizer vaccine - by far the most frequently used in Europe - have an 8 times higher chance of contracting the South African variant of the corona virus. 'We do it all for care' may now have exactly the opposite effect as more and more vaccinated people will need to be hospitalized.

In top vaccine nation Israel, the South African B.1.351 variant of the coronavirus is found in as many as 5.4% of Pfizer-vaccinated people. In unvaccinated people, it is only 0.7%. 'This means that this variant is able to break through the protection of the vaccine to some extent,' commented Adi Stern of the university.

Well, there is a much more logical explanation that numerous experts have already warned about, namely that the vaccine actually breaks down the natural resistance to virus mutations. Research points to the risk that it is precisely vaccines that can cause life-threatening mutations corona virus.

'Surprised by the outcome', but why?

Stern admitted that the scientific team was 'surprised' by the outcome. Of the 400 people studied, they had expected only one case of the South African variant, and not 8. 'Of course, I was not happy about that.'

However, it is a variant that occurs infrequently (1% of all assumed Covid cases), although this could change precisely because of the vaccine. After all: this mutation is hardly ever found in unvaccinated people, which means that the natural immune system is much better able to fight off this (supposed) virus. So, without vaccines, this harmless mutation would not have had a chance.

French university researchers noted in late February/early March that the Pfizer vaccine was causing mortality in Israel in all age groups to be tens to hundreds of times higher. The scientists were so shocked that they literally spoke of "a new Holocaust.

Despite this, unvaccinated people in Israel, and soon throughout Europe, are discriminated against and punished with partial exclusion from society. As we have written many times before, this too is part of the reversal of all values, norms, humanity and logic (light=darkness, darkness=light), which is so typical of a morally and mentally decaying civilization that is clearly hurtling ever faster towards the abyss.

Table of Contents

Chapter 1: Prepare the machine

Russia is busy defending itself and/or the Russian population in Ukraine in the event of an attack. Thus, these hypersonic Iskander missiles were deployed.

The mayor of the Russian city of Cherepovets (population 311,000+) has issued an ordinance to designate locations where "urgent" victims should be buried in time of war. The city is some 375 kilometers from Moscow, 800 kilometers from the border with Ukraine, and some 600 kilometers from the NATO countries of Estonia and Latvia. Why would a city deep in Russia take such a measure, other than to suggest that the Kremlin is indeed seriously preparing to have to fight a (world) war with the West? Russia has also warned that it will destroy two U.S. naval ships in the Black Sea if those ships are used in any military attack on Ukraine.

Resolution No. 1482, passed on April 5, deals with "the organization of urgent wartime burial of corpses" in the city of Cherepovets. The MKU (Center for Protection of Population and Territories in Emergency Situations) is responsible for designating, in cooperation with the federal government, places 'where bodies have been found, and to identify and document those who died in wartime.' It also procures "material and technical resources" for "the urgent burial of corpses and decontamination.

U.S. naval vessels may be destroyed

This ordinance in a city so deep in Russia can only mean that the country is seriously considering becoming the target of massive missile attacks, not only from Ukraine, but also from NATO territory, aircraft and ships.

For example, two U.S. destroyers are already sailing in the Black Sea. Dmitry Peskov, Kremlin press secretary, had a serious warning about this: 'If the cruise missiles of these destroyers are used against the territory of the Donetsk and Luhansk republics, these American warships can be destroyed. Russia will defend Russian citizens in this way.

Russia is not allowed by Merkel to respond to military provocations

NATO officials and Western politicians like Angela Merkel have ordered Russia to remove its troops - already 28 battalions in number - on the border with Ukraine. Has it now completely slipped the arrogant Western leaders' minds to forbid a country with historically the most determined military in the world to move troops on its own territory in response to the 110,000 troops Ukraine has amassed near the Russian-speaking cities of Luhansk and Donetsk?

It is Ukraine that cut off the supply of (drinking) water to Crimea after nearly 97% of the population decided in a referendum declared valid and fair by the OSCE to

return to the motherland Russia. If the Kiev regime
stops its shelling of Luhansk and Donetsk, withdraws its
troops, and removes the "temporary" dam at the
Dnieper allowing fresh water to flow back to the
Russian population, the issue can be resolved
diplomatically and peacefully.

But if the country necessarily wants war, then the
country will get war. Only let that NOT be with our
support. America and NATO should stay out of this.
There is no chance of that, however, since "war
president" Biden has already pledged his unabridged
support for Ukraine if an armed conflict breaks out.

On the other hand, even the allies know that
Washington's promises have been null and void for a
very long time. The United States, as a totally unhinged
empire, is imposing its will on the rest of the world with
outright blackmail and both economic and military
threats.

**Why does the West support a warmongering Neo-Nazi
regime?**

Ukrainian President and Western puppet Zelensky
recently signed a document stating that Crimea should
be conquered from Russia. This was nothing more than
a declaration of war by a regime, some of whose troops
would openly use Nazi flags in some places.

The message could hardly be clearer: America will militarily support Ukraine in the event of war. Is it very strange that the West is again associated in Russia with the Nazis, by whom they were betrayed at the time, and subsequently 20 million Russians died during WW2?

In any case, tensions with NATO are rising. According to unconfirmed reports, Polish and Belarusian border troops clashed recently. The past few weeks there have already been several exchanges of insults.

The Russian army has meanwhile set up a huge military camp with a field hospital some 250 kilometers from the border with Ukraine. More importantly, hypersonic Iskander missiles have been deployed, capable of carrying both a conventional and a nuclear warhead. Against these short-range missiles (500 km.) no defense is possible, for that they fly too fast (up to 2.6 km. per second). Moreover, the projectiles can change course during their flight and dodge defense missiles.

Analysts fear that a "hot" war may break out as early as May. Until then, European politicians should do everything they can to dissuade Ukraine and the US from further provocations, and resume talks with Russia. Unfortunately, 'our' leaders are too busy waging their own war against the freedom, self-determination, welfare and health of their own people.

Chapter 2: Keep the animals caged

After the Smart Mask the Smart Mark? With 'predictive programming', children have been brainwashed for years with the idea that everyone will soon have to have a mark in their hand/arm.

Besides the fact that part of the West is preparing for a new war, the population is being kept in check by measures concerning the corona virus. The possibility of pigeonholing the population and ensuring that we are gradually decimated is being approached in an increasingly creative manner. The World Economic Forum announces the next step towards total subordination and technocratic slavery: 'smart masks', which instruct you when you can breathe freely, whether the CO_2 level behind the mask is not too high, and even whether you are wearing the mask correctly. This insane plan, which will undoubtedly be "voluntary" at first but then mandatory anyway, underscores how totalitarian, anti-human and oppressive the global dictatorship now being imposed on the entire world population is becoming.

With a mortality rate of 0.037% established in official statistics, 'corona' is a deadly common respiratory virus of which the world has had hundreds, and from which 99% of people suffer little or no ill effects. As we have been writing and demonstrating for over a year, this crisis is not about a virus or public health at all, but about our subjugation to a global technocratic climate-vaccine dictatorship.

Facemasks are the symbol of total submission and inanity.

One of the most important symbols of will-less submission is the mouth mask, which has been shown to be useless and can even be very harmful, which was also openly acknowledged by politicians and experts for months, but which was then simply made mandatory anyway.

The virtually unopposed and uncritical swallowing of this utterly idiotic measure by almost the entire population was for the national and international 'Great Reset', 'Fourth Industrial Revolution' and 'Agenda 2030' planners the final confirmation that they could now do whatever they wanted, because the thinking capacity of most citizens appeared to have sunk far below the critical level of absolute inanity with the help of the mass media and flat entertainment.

Welcome to this global preschool

'This smart mask tells you when it needs to be washed,' the WEF begins its promotional video about BreathTech's oral diaper.

'And whether you are wearing it correctly. 'It measures your breathing rate, and if too much CO_2 has built up in it it tells you to take a few breaths of fresh air.' Well, since research has shown that CO2 levels are increased up to 1,000x after only a few minutes, that means you have to take your mouthguard off and on every few minutes throughout the day. Of course, that's never going to happen.

'And if you forget to put it on, it sets off an alarm.' How is that possible? Because, of course, the smart mask has to be linked to your smartphone, which in turn becomes part of the 4G/5G 'smart grid' that has been under construction for years, which will allow you to be tracked, monitored, instructed and corrected 24/7/365. The moment you put on the mouthpiece then, the smartphone will display a green symbol with the word "good. (Welcome to this global kindergarten classroom.)

The BreathTech S3 cap, as is the case with almost everything these days, is promoted as supposedly 'sustainable' and better for the environment. The manufacturer points out that mankind spent $166 billion on mouthguards last year, all of which ended up in landfills. Of course, this could have been easily avoided by simply never importing them. Finally, it has been shown that 'corona' in countries and states that did not introduce, or did away with, mouthguard requirements makes far fewer (supposed) sick and dead.

What is your idea for solving the world's biggest problems?

"What are your ideas for solving the world's biggest problems?" the video ends. Well, there can be no misunderstanding about that as far as I am concerned: if humanity still wants to have a free future, or a future at all, then first of all the WEF together with the Gates Foundation should be immediately targeted and banned as the greatest possible threat, and their leaders prosecuted in a new Nuremberg tribunal for serious crimes against humanity.

If not, the Smart Mask could well be succeeded by the Smart Mark, which could consist of an under-the-skin, externally scannable tattoo and/or vaccines with nano-biosensors that not only prove that you have been vaccinated, but also contain all your personal data, simultaneously becoming your ID card and debit card.

This 'mark of the beast' system via vaccinations - which Netflix showed as early as 2017 in the children's cartoon 'Stretch Armstrong & The Flex Fighters - we first described in 2009 and is now on the verge of being implemented globally with increasingly compelling measures.

13

Chapter 3: RNA fraud

CDC sued for massive fraud: Tests at 7 universities of ALL people examined showed that they did not have Covid, but just Influenza A or B - RIVM and EU statistics: 'Corona' virtually disappeared, even under mortality.

A clinical scientist and immunologist-virologist at a southern California laboratory says he and colleagues from 7 universities are suing the CDC for massive fraud. The reason: not one of 1500 samples of people tested "positive" could find Covid-19. ALL people were simply found to have Influenza A, and to a lesser extent Influenza B. This is consistent with the previous findings of other scientists, which we have reported on several times.

Dr. Derek Knauss: "When my lab team and I subjected the 1500 supposedly positive Covid-19 samples to Koch's postulates and put them under an SEM (electron microscope), we found NO Covid in all 1500 samples. We found that all 1500 samples were primarily Influenza A, and some Influenza B, but no cases of Covid. We did not use the worthless PCR tests.'

Covid has not been discovered once at 7 universities in recent times

'When we sent the rest of the samples to Stanford, Cornell, and a couple of the labs at the University of

California, they came up with the same result: NO COVID. They found Influenza A and B. Then we all asked the CDC for viable samples of Covid. The CDC said they can't give them, because they don't have those samples.'

'So, we came to the hard conclusion through all our research and lab work that Covid-19 was imaginary and fictitious. The flu was only called 'Covid,' and most of the 225,000 deaths were from co-morbidities such as heart disease, cancer, diabetes, pulmonary emphysema, etc... They got the flu which further weakened their immune systems, and they died.'

This virus is fictitious

'I still need to find one viable sample with Covid-19 to work with. We who conducted the lab test with these 1500 samples at the 7 universities are now suing the CDC for Covid-19 fraud. The CDC still has not sent us a viable, isolated and purified sample of Covid-19. If they can't or won't, then I say there is no Covid-19. It's fictional.'

'The four research papers describing the genome extracts of the Covid-19 virus never managed to isolate and purify the samples. All four papers describe only small pieces of RNA that are only 37 to 40 base pairs long. That is NOT a VIRUS. A viral genome normally has 30,000 to 40,000 base pairs.'

'Now that Covid-19 is supposedly so bad everywhere, how come not one lab in the world has completely isolated and purified this virus? That's because they never really found the virus. All they ever discovered were small pieces of RNA that were not identified as the virus anyway. So, what we're dealing with is just another flu strain, just like every year. Covid-19 does not exist and is fictitious.'

'I believe that China and the globalists have set up this Covid hoax (the flu disguised as a new virus) to establish a global tyranny and totalitarian control police state. This intrigue included (also) massive election fraud to overthrow Trump.'

'The detection of viral RNA cannot demonstrate the presence of an infectious virus, or that 2019-nCoV is the causative agent of clinical symptoms.' And furthermore: 'This test cannot rule out other diseases caused by other bacterial or viral pathogens.'

In other words, we cannot prove that the people who get sick and are hospitalized, and very occasionally die, were sickened by a new coronavirus called SARS-CoV-2, nor can we prove that it caused them to develop a new disease called 'Covid-19.' It could just as easily be a different virus and a different disease. (And since all the symptoms, including severe pneumonia, are seamlessly similar to what flu can cause historically in vulnerable people... 'if it looks like a duck and walks like a duck, it is a duck'.

Reward of €225,000 for demonstrating coronavirus

Earlier this year, Samuel Eckert's German Team and the Isolate Truth Fund offered a reward of at least €225,000 for any scientist who can provide incontrovertible proof that the SARS-CoV-2 virus has been isolated and therefore exists. They too pointed out that not one lab in the world has yet been able to isolate this corona virus.

Yes, systems scientists claim they have, but this 'isolation' consists only of a sample from the human body, which is a 'soup' full of different kinds of cells, remains of viruses, bacteria, et cetera. With the help of (toxic) chemicals one then searches for some (residual) particles that may indicate a virus that once existed or may still exist, after which this is designated as 'evidence'.

Canadian team also found no evidence despite 40 WOB requests

In late December 2020, we paid attention to a similar initiative like the one in Germany. A team around Canadian investigative journalist Christine Massey submitted to medical authorities worldwide no less than 40 WOB requests simply asking for proof that the SARS-CoV-2 virus has been isolated, and its existence can therefore be objectively proven. Not one of the agencies and authorities written to was able to provide that evidence.

'Impossible to show that SARS-CoV-2 causes a disease called Covid-19'

Dr. Tom Cowan, Dr. Andrew Kaufman and Sally Fallon Morell recently published a statement on "the continuing controversy over whether the SARS-CoV-2 virus is isolated or purified. But based on the official Oxford definition of "isolation" ("the fact or condition of being isolated or secluded, a separation from other things or persons, standing alone"), common sense, the laws of logic and the rules of science dictate that any unbiased person must come to the conclusion that the SARS-CoV-2 virus has never been isolated or purified. As a result, no confirmation of the existence of the virus can be given.'

'The logical and scientific implications of this fact are that the structure and composition of something whose existence cannot be proven cannot be known, including the presence, structure and function of hypothetical spike or other proteins. The genetic sequence of something that has never been found cannot be known, nor can the "variants" (mutations) of something whose existence has not been demonstrated. It is therefore impossible to show that SARS-CoV-2 causes a disease called Covid-19.'

Combined PCR test for corona and influenza 'because there's hardly any difference'

The world's largest biotech company, the Chinese BGI, has recently introduced a new PCR test that can simultaneously test for influenza A, B and corona.

Apart from the proven fact, that a PCR test cannot prove infection with any virus whatsoever, BGI's explanation that both diseases are so difficult to distinguish from each other and that they have therefore made only one test, says more than enough. Maybe there IS no difference at all, 'Covid' is just another name for 'old familiar' flu viruses, and this is just another clever marketing trick?

With the government-sanctioned 24/7 fear propaganda by the mass media, most people have come to believe that there is indeed a life-threatening virus that makes people sick much faster and more severely than seasonal flu. However, even the latter is demonstrably not the case. Influenza A has been the leading cause of death from pneumonia in the developed world for years.

But send people designated as severe Covid patients to a few ICUs around the country, put cameras on them constantly, instruct a few physicians that they should only discuss the worst cases, and you have your "televised pandemic. The argument 'we are doing it because otherwise care will be overburdened' was undermined by the government itself some time ago by rejecting an offer of 400 ICU beds plus staff because 'it is not necessary'. (Was this perhaps the first and only time the truth was told?)

Nothing more to worry about (yet it never gets back to normal)

Now that also the official figures of the RIVM show that after the normal traditional winter peak nothing is wrong, and according to the EU statistics (EuroMOMO) there is even a significant underdevelopment, society - if it really was about a virus and public health - should immediately go back to normal to start repairing the huge damage caused by government policies.

However, as you know, that will never be done, and that is because this carefully planned pandemic hoax is carrying out an ideological agenda, the 'Great Reset', which aims to largely demolish the society and economy of the West, and then subject it to a global technocratic communist climate-vaccine dictatorship, in which all our freedoms, civil and self-determination rights will be done away with once and for all.

Chapter 4: Shameless concealment?

85% of all people who died (supposedly) of Covid-19 could have been alive today if politics and the media had not done everything, they could to suppress existing drugs. This is not just anyone saying this, but one of the world's top medics, Professor Dr. Peter McCullough, who is the world's most published expert in his field. McCullough pointed out these shocking facts in a statement to the Texas State Assembly Committee on Public Health and Human Services. In our view, the deliberate withholding of proven working and safe medications amounts to a gross crime against humanity, and is in fact tantamount to an indirect form of genocide.

McCullough is an internist, cardiologist and medical professor at the Health Sciences Center at Texas A&M University. He is the most published expert in his field in history, as well as editor of two major medical journals.

Absolutely stunned' that the public is being denied working treatments

He said he was "absolutely flabbergasted" that not one of the 50,000 peer-reviewed papers on Covid-19 mentioned a treatment (other than vaccinations). Together with a team of experts, he did conduct such a study, and subsequently came up with an excellent treatment, which was published in the authoritative American Journal of Medicine. They also made a

YouTube video of it, which immediately went viral - until YouTube blocked it within a week.

'Unbelievable what was done,' the professor continued. 'How many of you have ever heard on TV or radio that home treatment is possible? Even one word about what to do (with medication) if you are diagnosed with Covid-19? This is a complete and total failure in every area! Why no panel of doctors to prevent as many hospitalizations as possible? Why no reports of treated patients who did not have to go to the hospital as a result? It is a total travesty that you do not treat a fatal disease.' He therefore called for every test result to be accompanied by a treatment recommendation as standard from now on.

Countries that did allow medication to have only 1% to 10% of the number of deaths

The professor pointed out that countries outside the West that did allow these drugs (such as HCQ/zinc protocol, Quercetin, Ivermectin) had proportionally only 1% to 10% of the 'First World' deaths. 'But when was the last time you turned on the news and got an update on this? When did you get an update on how the rest of the world is dealing with Covid?'

Just as in Europe, in the US there are only a handful of the same doctors and 'experts' who paint the same extremely one-sided, distorted, misleading picture on TV every time, designed to keep the entire population in a state of mortal fear (and therefore absolute obedience to most absurd measures). Not one of these doctors and experts ever mentions that Covid patients can be treated and cured easily, quickly and very safely with existing medication.

80% group immunity, mass vaccinations totally unnecessary

It is estimated that Texas, where almost all corona measures were lifted on March 1 and life is almost back to normal - and corona is also almost gone - now has 80% group immunity. People who get Covid and build up antibodies to it, "have complete and long-term immunity. You can't beat that. You can't make that better with vaccines. There are no scientific, clinical or safety arguments for ever vaccinating or testing a recovered Covid patient.'

During the vaccine testing phases last year, only less than 1% of the placebo group actually received Covid-19, McCullough reiterates based on official reports. 'But the vaccine is going to have an impact of at least 1% on public health. That's what the data says. The vaccine is not going to save us, and we already have 80% group immunity.'

Vaccines should only be given strategically to a few vulnerable groups, he believes. However, people up to the age of 50 with reasonable health definitely do not need to be vaccinated. 'There is no scientific argument for that.' One of the biggest fallacies for vaccinations is so-called 'asymptomatic spread'. 'I want to be very clear about that: there is hardly any such thing, if it exists at all. A sick person passes it on to a sick person. The Chinese published a study ... to 11 million people. They were trying to find evidence of asymptomatic spread. It's not there. It's one of the most important pieces of misinformation.

'85% deaths and hospitalizations could easily have been prevented'

The professor emphasized that suppressing information about effective and safe treatments has been enormously harmful. Two 'very large' studies have shown that 'if doctors treat their 50-plus patients with medical problems in a timely manner with a multi-drug protocol... there are 85% fewer hospitalizations and deaths.'

'We have over 500,000 deaths in the US. We could have prevented 85% (425,000) of those if our response to the pandemic had been razor-sharply focused on the problem that is right in front of our eyes: the sick patient.'

French professor Christian Perronne, with a very impressive track record, published his book last year with the telling title 'Is There a Mistake They Didn't Make? - Covid-19: The sacred union of incompetence and arrogance.' If corona patients had been treated from the outset (especially preventively) with zinc, hydroxychloroquine/quercetin, vitamins C and D, and azithromycin, there would have been hardly any deaths, and 25,000 French people (80% of the death toll at the time) would still be alive today, according to him.

It would just be your child, (grand)parent, partner, friend or colleague who has been put on the list of victims of a gross crime against humanity in this disgraceful manner, of an indirect genocide even, sacrificed on the altar of the transhuman ideology that everyone should be injected with these gene-manipulating "vaccines" no matter what, and no other means should jeopardize that perfidious intention.

Chapter 5: Cyber attacks

In 2021-2022, on the ruins of the current system, the long-planned new all-digital system, a communist-fascist technocracy, will be established

Just as a 'live' exercise was held in October 2019 with a corona pandemic (Event 201), then actually carried out three months later, so Klaus Schwab's World Economic Forum will 'simulate' a massive cyber-attack in the summer. Cyber Polygon 2021 will take place on July 9, 2021, and is intended - as with corona and Event 201 - to set up a detailed script for what will actually be carried out some time later (possibly as early as the fall): a massive 'attack' on the digital and energy infrastructure, which should bring the West in particular to its knees once and for all before the Great Reset.

Digital globalization has connected the world so tightly that malicious individuals can use cyber and hacking attacks to cause major damage to the financial system, energy supplies, businesses and infrastructure, the WEF warns. The entire modern society has become so dependent on this that a few days without access to banks and payments, or worse, without electricity and water, will be enough to cause total panic.

Why are the Russians participating?

Who will be blamed for this monstrous false flag operation is unclear. The obvious one is the time-honored, hackneyed excuse "the Russians did it! But Russia's largest state-owned bank, Sberbank, along with its cyber division BIZONE, is actually participating in Cyber Polygon 2021.

What is going on here? Is Russia perhaps in the same plot by the WEF to bring the West to its knees once and for all? Or are the Russians participating in Cyber Polygon 2021 because top U.S. politicians and military officials have been openly threatening a cyber-attack on Russia for years. If that is the real reason, then it would be smart to make yourself as aware as possible of the enemy's methods so that you can arm yourself against them.

Financial mega-crisis in 2021-2022

For years we have been warning of an inevitable financial mega-crisis, because the Western - and especially European - banking system is technically bankrupt, the still rapidly growing debt burden has become unsustainable, the euro only has value on paper, and the years of negative interest rates of the ECB have completely eroded savings, pensions and purchasing power of the euro. We are therefore living 'on borrowed time', or rather: time bought with enormous amounts of new digital money (tens of billions per month), which has only delayed the big blow (and which, partly because of this, will be much harder, and will probably be a fact in 2021-2022).

Since that mega systemic crisis is now very close, the governments, banks and big financial players need a scapegoat for their planned "false flag" attack, which will give the dying system a "controlled" final blow before it collapses on its own. The mess caused by the collapse will be so huge and will claim so many victims that hundreds of millions of desperate people will want to take out their anger on the real culprits, in this case the same governments and banks, led by large globalist organizations, with the WEF at the helm.

Who will be the scapegoat?

In order to prevent uprisings and revolutions it is 'necessary' that the population be given a scapegoat. Perhaps that will be another group of Russian, Chinese or Eastern European hackers. China might suit the U.S. very well, as the Pentagon is also planning a 'hot' war against that country in the near future. Iran and North Korea could also be mentioned, perhaps even cooperating with China in a new so-called 'axis of evil', which would then have to be countered 'naturally'.

Or is the enmity with China just a sham, meant to further fuel popular fears of war and other calamities? After all, both the US and the EU are busy copying the totalitarian Chinese control system.

Another option is for the false flag cyber-attack to be traced to Israel, which NATO and the UN Security Council will use to force the military-threatened country to agree to a "peace plan" that will split the country in two and make Jerusalem some kind of international city. We showed in several articles more than 10 years ago that the Vatican and Freemasonry have been setting their sights on Jerusalem for a very long time, because they want to make it the center of some kind of merged new world religion.

Anyway, the corona pandemic hoax has shown unequivocally that it cannot be presented as so crazy or improbable, or the staggeringly uninformed, uninterested and inebriated Western population blindly accepts it. EVERYTHING governments and media claim is now believed, "because they said it on TV, and so it's true.

Communist-fascist technocracy in which even your body no longer belongs to you

The Great Reset of the WEF has begun since last year to break down and radically change our society. The last remnants of freedom, democracy and self-determination will disappear for good, cash will be replaced by fully digital currencies, and the new 'stakeholder capitalism' is nothing but a combined communist-fascist system in which truly everything will be taken away from citizens and companies, even the right to control your own body.

The state essentially becomes sole major shareholder of really every aspect of total life. Initially, it will get more than enough popular support for this, because this system provides for the advent of a Universal Basic Income, and the aforementioned planned cyber-attack will create so much chaos and misery, that people will accept any solution uncritically and even with the greatest enthusiasm. ("Ordo ab Chao")

But soon the survivors of the coming world crisis will find that in the new system they will have absolutely nothing and no say, not even over their own bodies. With one mandatory mRNA vaccination after another - possibly soon containing nano-chips - they will turn into genetically engineered digital slaves, into a kind of androids or cyborgs. Klaus Schwab has literally announced mandatory brain scans and chips that will allow even your thoughts, desires and your will to be controlled and manipulated.

WEF threatens survival of humanity; therefore, a true Great Reset is needed

The World Economic Forum thus unambiguously presents itself as one of the greatest threats to the survival of humanity. It is quite conceivable that the WEF, with the support of the Western powers, will come a long way, but in the end, we suspect, this most horrible anti-human dictatorship will not last long. In their boundless arrogance, they think they can control and change human nature, but what they will create is nothing short of hell on earth, which will completely consume itself under the weight of its own megalomaniac malignancy.

Then it will finally be time for a real Great Reset, one that believers say will be carried out "from on high. That kingdom of peace will last for all eternity, and will no longer accommodate figures such as Klaus Schwab, Bill Gates, George Soros and Mark Zuckerberg, nor the banking elite still above them led by the infamous Rothschild family. That "Babylon" will have been permanently destroyed, never to rise again to terrorize humanity.

Chapter 6: The great reset

The "Great Reset" was designed to prolong the current dying system, but will not work'

Years ago, we first paid attention to the gloomy forecasts of the private geopolitical and military intelligence site Deagel.com, which relies on official figures, reports and documents from the CIA, the US Department of Defense, the World Bank, the WEF, the EU, the IMF, and just about every conceivable authoritative international body and organization, among others. In the analysis updated in September 2020, nothing actually appears to have changed: in 2025, the West is still in total collapse, although the severity of the blow varies from country to country. The U.S., Great Britain and Germany will suffer particularly badly, while the Netherlands and Finland will be the least affected in Europe. Nevertheless, Deagel expects that around 1 million people will also disappear in our country.

In 2014, Deagel wrote that as a result of unlimited money printing and debt, the Western bloc on both sides of the ocean will have collapsed by 2025. That fate is still inevitable. Moreover, the corona crisis has shown that "the success model of the Western world is built on societies without resilience, which can hardly tolerate any adversity, even of low intensity. We assumed that, and we now have, without a doubt, the full confirmation of that.'

Great Reset: temporary extension of a dying system

'The Covid crisis will be used to extend the life of this dying economic system through the so-called Great Reset, which like the climate change, extinction rebellion, planetary crisis, 'green revolution' and shale oil hoaxes is being promoted by the system.'

And just as with the corona lockdowns and the deliberate destruction of the hospitality industry, tourism and much of the SME sector, everything about the 'Great Reset' is aimed at turning back the consumption economy sharply so that we can continue on more or less the same footing for a few more years. 'That may be effective for a while, but will not solve the core problem, and will only postpone the inevitable. The ruling elite hopes to stay in power, which is in fact all they really care about.'

Covid has shown that the West can no longer deal with hardship

'The collapse of the Western financial system - and ultimately Western civilization - through a confluence of crises is the key element in the forecast, and has a devastating outcome. Covid has shown that Western societies that have embraced multiculturalism and extreme liberalism are incapable of dealing with real adversity.'

As a striking example, Deagel gives the Spanish flu pandemic of about a century ago. It claimed the lives of some 40-50 million people. Now the world's population is four times larger, and if corona were just as bad, it would have killed at least 160 million to 200 million people (given globalism and intensive air travel, twice that is more likely). But the (most likely artificially highly inflated) death toll currently stands at 2.9 million, or only 0.037% of the world's population, which is comparable to a mild seasonal flu wave.

Most prosperous states will pay the highest price

'It is very likely that the economic crisis resulting from the lockdowns will cause more deaths than the virus worldwide,' Deagel therefore argues. 'The stark reality of diverse and multicultural Western societies is that a collapse - depending on various factors - will take a toll of 50% to 80% (of the population). Overall, the most diverse, multicultural, indebted welfare states (with the highest standards of living) will pay the heaviest price.'

The only thing that still holds our abnormal, errant Western society together like "glue" is "overconsumption, with high doses of unlimited degeneracy packaged as virtue. Despite widespread censorship, 'hate laws' and contradictory signals show that even this glue no longer works. But not everyone has to die; migration can also play a positive role in this.'

Second- and Third-World countries that cling to the "Old World Order" will go down with the West, analysts expect. But because these countries are poorer, the blow will be much less severe. Moreover, these are often still homogeneous (cohesive) societies, historically much more resilient to a major systemic crisis or other calamity. Countries that turn to China have the greatest chance of stabilizing quickly again.

Now that the EU has for years rejected any rapprochement with Russia and has even begun to portray it as an enemy, Russia and China have begun to form a strategic economic and military alliance (which will replace the West and form the true New World Order). Contrary to what is claimed in the West, not only Russia but also China is already far ahead of America and Europe (/ NATO) with military technology in many areas.

A new major (world) war is even called "the most likely major event" in these 20s. The first scenario is a conventional war (as is about to break out in Ukraine) escalating to a nuclear war. The second scenario is placed between 2025 and 2030, and assumes an overwhelming Russian surprise attack on the West. To the dismay of the Western military elite, the Russians showed in Syria in 2015 that they are capable of carrying out such an attack to perfection at a distance of more than 2,000 kilometers.

'The irony is that since the end of the Cold War, the US has put NATO in position to carry out such a 'first strike' on Russia, and it now looks like that first strike is indeed going to happen, but the country that will be finished off is the US.'

Westerners are brainwashed and arrogant

Another peculiarity of the Western system is that its subjects have been brainwashed to the point where the majority have come to take their moral supremacy and technological edge for granted. This has paved the way for the supremacy of emotional arguments over rational ones, which are ignored or belittled *(this is now true in ALL areas, be it climate, energy, immigration, economics, Russia or corona)*. This mindset may play a key role in the upcoming catastrophic events.'

At least the silent majority of the population in the former Soviet Union was still aware of their shortcomings, which they had, once had clean enough of. Westerners, and certainly Americans, however, think of themselves as only tremendously clever and far above the rest. Now America and Europe are claiming that Russia and China are stealing all kinds of technologies from them, "which proves that now the Western elite is also infected with this hubris. In the next decade it will become clear that the West is lagging behind the Russia-China bloc, after which malaise (in the West) may turn to despair.'

'Starting a war seems like a quick and easy solution to restore lost supremacy. In 1940, France had no nuclear weapons to turn defeat into victory. The West might try this now, because of the unpleasant prospect that we will be 'the tyrant and his filthy whore' (*a very apt description of the US and Europe*) who will fearfully flee while the rest of the world laughs at them.'

'If there is no dramatic change of course, the world will definitely witness the first nuclear war. The collapse of the Western bloc may occur before, during or after that war. It doesn't matter. A nuclear war is a gamble with billions of casualties, and during the collapse the number will be in the hundreds of millions.'

Russia rises to the top

The only two countries in Europe where the blow will be less severe are the Netherlands and Finland. In the Netherlands, the population declines by about 1 million people to 16 million (-6%), and purchasing power comes to $47,451, only 7% less than the current $51,200. Finland does even better with a population decline of 5% and a purchasing power decline of 1%.

The country with the greatest wealth growth is Russia, where residents will see their purchasing power rise by a whopping 63% to $43,557. This puts Russia in 5th place, behind Brunei, Qatar, Singapore and the Netherlands. China, with a 48th place on the list and a purchasing power of only $17,843, surprisingly does much less well than would be expected.

Given the enormous enthusiasm of the European neoliberals (in view of their policies, the term neo-Marxists is more appropriate) for the Great Reset and the EU superstate, I fear that the comparatively still reasonable expectations for Europeans may well prove misplaced. Nevertheless, there are encouraging signs in our society of growing resistance to the systemic politicians of Brussels, of whom it is becoming increasingly clear that they are only concerned with promoting their own interests at the expense of the welfare, prosperity and future of our people.

Chapter 7: The next step

The deliberately sown fear of death over a common respiratory virus seems to have turned countless people into utterly submissive, mindless zombies since last year.

According to a study of Covid mRNA vaccines published by the Human Microbiology Institute, it now appears that this may literally be happening. Indeed, the vaccines that use mRNA to encode the Spike protein of the original SARS-CoV-2 in your own body appear to be able to cause very serious neurological disorders, including ALS, Creutzfeld-Jakob (also known as "mad cow disease") and Alzheimer's disease. Creutzfeld-Jakob (CJD) is 100% fatal.

The mRNA in the vaccines from Pfizer, AstraZeneca and Moderna 'hijack' your body cells in a fairly random way, and then prompt them to make the Spike protein from the coronavirus. Thus, these 'vaccines' are in reality not vaccines at all, but gene therapy, or genetic manipulation of the human body.

The monstrously expensive 'Green Deal' poses enormous risks to prosperity, the economy and democracy, according to DB. Those risks should be told honestly to the people, and not withheld, as is happening now. At least that is what Eric Heymann, senior economist at Deutsche Bank Research, writes.

Prions cause ALS, Creutzfeld-Jakob and Alzheimer's disease

The Spike protein contains "prion-like regions" that allow it to bind particularly well to human ACE2 receptors. Prions are proteinaceous infectious particles that are the cause of a number of deadly brain diseases in both humans and animals.

If the human immune system attacks the mRNA sequences in the vaccine before it reaches its destination, prions can be released into the body, warns the study's author, J. Bart Classen (MD) of Classen Immunotherapies Inc. in Manchester, UK. The DNA-binding protein TDP-43 and the FUS gene (which instructs the body to make protein) can be affected by prions. This process has been scientifically established to cause the dreaded diseases ALS, Creutzfeld-Jakob and Alzheimer's, as well as other serious neurological disorders.

The mRNA in the vaccines from Pfizer, AstraZeneca and Moderna 'hijack' your body cells in a fairly random way, and then prompt them to make the Spike protein of the coronavirus. Thus, these 'vaccines' are in reality not vaccines at all, but gene therapy, or genetic manipulation of the human body.

Prions cause ALS, Creutzfeld-Jakob and Alzheimer's disease

The Spike protein contains "prion-like regions" that allow it to bind particularly well to human ACE2 receptors. Prions are proteinaceous infectious particles that are the cause of a number of deadly brain diseases in both humans and animals.

If the human immune system attacks the mRNA sequences in the vaccine before it reaches its destination, prions can be released into the body, warns the study's author, J. Bart Classen (MD) of Classen Immunotherapies Inc. in Manchester, UK. The DNA-binding protein TDP-43 and the FUS gene (which instructs the body to make protein) can be affected by prions. This process has been scientifically established to cause the dreaded diseases ALS, Creutzfeld-Jakob and Alzheimer's, as well as other serious neurological disorders.

Does the world await (tens of) millions of severe neurological patients?

Creutzfeld-Jakob (mad cow disease) is 100% fatal. The disease is irreversible, and there is no treatment for it. Symptoms are consistent with brain hemorrhages, and manifest as confusion, difficulty speaking, strange body movements, emotional and personality changes, and a major loss of cognitive function, ending with death, among others. Once the prions are active and begin to cause these symptoms, it is too late.

There is therefore a danger that corona mRNA vaccines will cause an unprecedented wave of severe neurological disease in the coming years. In millions or even tens of millions of people, the brain may be slowly "eaten" by prions*, causing dementia, inability to function, and eventually, inability to think. Not to mention, in the meantime, will suffer worse and worse.

Vaccinzombies

As we have been writing for almost a year now, almost all vaccine-induced illnesses, diseases and deaths will automatically be attributed to mutations, new viruses or 'coincidences' for which the pharmaceutical industry has developed a new vaccine. You will never hear or read this in the mainstream fake news media; they only quote 'us scientists and 'experts' who - regardless of the misery created - will continue to claim that these vaccines are 'perfectly safe'. So, Baghdad Bob on repeat, only worldwide with lots of copies.

CNBC already reported that 1 in 3 Covid 'survivors' suffer from a mental or psychological disorder such as dementia, depression or anxiety disorders. Is this really caused by an ordinary respiratory virus, or 'secretly' by the vaccines? A mysterious brain-damaging disease has already surfaced in Canada whose symptoms are suspiciously similar to the prion-induced conditions mentioned above (memory loss, hallucinations, muscle atrophy). Doctors say it is not Creutzfeld-Jakob, but they have not yet found another cause.

Will the successful horror series 'The Walking Dead' become reality in a slightly different way in the coming years as the world is overrun with 'vaccine zombies'? Given the tidal wave of serious side effects and deaths that are already occurring, this no longer seems like pure fantasy.

So, if you're still planning on going to a vaccine drive...

Here's to your health!

Chapter 8: One way or the other

*'Do as many tasks as possible without a mouth mask on,
and avoid physical exertion if you do wear one'*

The fact that mouthguards are useless and can cause
significant health damage has now been extensively
demonstrated. What was not yet known was that
frequent wearing of mouth caps can cause eye damage.
At least that is what a team of Chinese scientists has
found. Their study was published in March 2021 in the
scientific journal Translational Vision Science &
Technology.

Another journal, The Review of Optometry, provided a
summary of this study. Chinese scientists investigated
the effects of wearing mouthguards during physically
strenuous activities. 23 healthy young adults were given
different types of mouthguards to wear during a
running test. The speed was gradually increased until
they reached a heart rate of 190 bpm.

The participants were divided into three groups:
without a mouthguard, with a medical mouthguard (the
familiar blue one) and with an N95 mouthguard. Before
and after the test, a scan was made of the optic nerves
and vessels in the retina of the eye.

Even before the test, the N95 wearers were already
found to have significantly reduced blood vessel density
compared to those who did not wear a mouthguard.

Potential damage to retina, impaired performance, breathlessness, low oxygen saturation

Afterwards, both groups of mouthguard wearers were found to have run for less time and the oxygen saturation in their blood was sharply reduced, as was the vascular density in their retinas.

The scientists found that the N95 mouthguard in particular causes this effect even in a quiescent state, which could have potential retinal damage and other clinical implications for healthcare workers and other professions who must wear mouthguards for long periods of time every day.

All volunteers wearing mouthguards reached the maximum heart rate of 190 bpm much faster and had significantly lower oxygen saturation in their blood afterward than the non-wearers. An earlier walking test had already shown that wearing the medical (blue) mouth caps leads to dyspnea (shortness of breath) within 6 minutes.

Advice: wear as little mouth protection as possible

The conclusion is that mouthguards delay the return to a normal heart rate after exercise, reduce performance during exercises and sports, make wearers less attentive to injuries, and cause hypoxemia (abnormally low oxygen level in the blood). The scientists therefore advise everyone to perform as many tasks as possible without mouthguards, and to avoid physical exertion while wearing mouthguards.

Effect nil, supposed effect already gone after 10-15 minutes

A Washington Post article admitted that wearing mouthguards during the Spanish flu pandemic over a century ago had no effect whatsoever. Recent studies of mouthguards in Denmark and the US, the largest ever conducted, also concluded that the effect of mouthguards is nil at best, and only gives the wearers a (false) sense of security.

In any case, it has already been established that the N95 caps are saturated with the moisture in your breath after a maximum of 20 minutes, and the blue caps after only 10-15 minutes, and therefore completely lose their supposed effect.

German professor: Mouthguards can actually strengthen infections

The authoritative German pathology professor Dr. Arne Burkhardt explained in a 50-page report the devastating effects of wearing mouthguards on our health, and therefore does not counteract the so-called "pandemic" but seems to perpetuate it.

Burkhardt warned that the prolonged wearing of mouthguards is highly damaging to the facial skin,

46

respiratory tract, lungs and the total human organism, and can lead to numerous diseases and disorders. There is also evidence that viral, bacterial and fungal infections are promoted by mouthguards, and people can actually infect themselves through them.

Health Canada and the Quebec provincial government recently advised schools to immediately stop wearing and distributing medical (blue) mouthguards because they contain microscopic graphene particles that can get into the lungs, and then cause serious damage just like asbestos.

Chapter 9: Vaccine tiranny

No jab, no job: Employers may start requiring vaccinations from their employees

The European Court of 'Human Rights' (ECHR) has ruled that mandatory vaccinations are legal. This shocking, outrageous decision destroys the integrity of your own body and paves the way for the biggest human rights violation ever, mandatory corona vaccinations. It underlines that also the European judicial system is rotten and corrupt, and only serves the interests of pharma and tech multinationals, plus of course the politicians who have been bribed or bought by them.

The decision by the "judges" followed a complaint by a group of Czech families who had been fined and whose children were not allowed to attend nurseries because they had not had the obligatory vaccinations against nine diseases (including diphtheria, tetanus, whooping cough, hepatitis B and measles).

According to the parents, the obligation goes against Article 8 on the right to respect for personal life, but the Court disagreed, stating that the vaccinations are "in the best interest" of the children so that "every child is protected against serious diseases by vaccinations or group immunity.

Road clear for mandatory vaccinations and corona passports

'Compulsory vaccinations can be considered necessary in a democratic society,' the European judges said. Although this judgment was not directly about Covid, in the very near future it could have extremely far-reaching consequences for every citizen. In addition to compulsory vaccinations, this also paves the way for compulsory vaccine passports, which will be required to gain access to catering and events, and later also to agencies, institutions and businesses (no jab = no job).

Indeed, according to ECHR law expert Nicolas Hervieu, the decision ratifies the efforts of European politicians to make Covid vaccinations mandatory. (For inveterate vaccine proponents, read for example 13-09: Pharma giant Pfizer blames anti-vaxxers if vaccines fail to stop corona (/ Vaccine proponents use twisted and contradictory logic to force others to get vaccinated too - 'But measles, whooping cough and polio have all but disappeared because of vaccines, haven't they?').

System of 'the Beast' another step closer

Suffice it to conclude this message once again with the well-known Biblical prophecy in which (based on the source text) is described exactly what will be done in the coming years and where it will lead, if not enough people are willing to do everything possible to stop the

49

coming of this profoundly anti-human, diabolical system.

AstraZeneca has changed the name of its genetically engineered "chimpanzee" vaccine to Vaxzevria, possibly to divert attention from the fact that people everywhere continue to die after being injected with this highly experimental, patently dangerous substance. The package insert for the AZ/Vaxzevria vaccine is already so terrifying that it is unthinkable for people with half a functioning mind to ever be injected with it. Despite this, the administration of this vaccine in the Europe, which in my personal opinion amounts to a potentially serious crime against humanity, has only been temporarily suspended.

Augusta Turiaco, 55, and Cinzia Pennino, 46, can be added to the ever-growing list of corona vaccine fatalities. Both teachers became deathly ill within days of being injected with the AZ vaccine, were found to have developed blood clots, and died within one to two weeks. Despite this, authorities claimed that there was "no connection" to the vaccine.

Young German woman dies after vaccine, politician says 'on the take'

32-year-old German psychologist Dana Ottman became deathly ill immediately after her AZ vaccination. Less than two weeks later, she was found dead in bed by her mother. Cause of death: a massive brain hemorrhage. A doctor says from behind his hand that the vaccine is most likely the cause. Then she hears an SPD politician on TV chillingly declare that "we have to put up with 'the few people' who die from the vaccines". Easy to say, if it's not your own daughter or other loved one.

Nevertheless, Germany decided not to use the vaccine for the time being for people up to the age of 60. Shortly thereafter, Europe mostly suspended administration of the AZ stuff for everyone, but only temporarily for now. Now that a new name has been put on it, Vaxzevria, vaccination is likely to resume as usual soon. After all, Minister De Jonge has attached his name and reputation to it, and has poured hundreds of millions of government money into it.

'Genetically engineered chimpanzee adenovirus grown in human embryonic cells'

One look at the package insert for this vaccine, however, should make any right-thinking person shudder in horror: 'Contains a chimpanzee-derived genetically engineered adenovirus grown in human embryonic kidney cells. This product contains genetically altered organisms (GVOs).'('One dose (0.5 ml) contains no less than 250 million infectious units of chimpanzee adenovirus, which encodes the SARS-CoV-2 spike glycoprotein ChAdOx1-S.' - page 2 and page.19).

Despite this, the media and politicians continue to insist that genetic engineering and human 'abortion cells' are a 'conspiracy theory', when it is noted in black and white in the manufacturers' own documentation. (As we have already shown with regard to the Pfizer vaccine.) What is not described is that the foreign DNA from the 'monkey' adenovirus can be seen as foreign by our immune system, which can cause serious auto-immune reactions in the long term, even years after administration.

Barely noticeable difference in test phases

The leaflet further states that in the test phase the difference between the vaccinated group and the control group, both containing over 5000 people, is extremely small. Of the 5258 vaccinated, 64 people (1.2%) still received Covid-19, and of the 5210 in the control group, 154 (3.0%). Efficacy averaged 59.5% within 4 to 12 weeks. In fact, the difference between participants 56 to 65 years old was only one person (8 people in the Vaxzevria, and 9 people in the control group received Covid-19).

Note that these are also manufacturer-performed "the butcher inspecting his own meat" tests. People who have already had corona, or who suffer from a variety of serious conditions (cardiovascular, intestinal, liver, kidney, endocrine/metabolic, neurological) were NOT tested, but in practice are WELL vaccinated. Then we leave aside the established fact that the PCR tests used produce 90% to 98% false positives.

Effects on frail and pregnant people NOT studied

The package insert goes on to state that there have indeed been "some cases" of deaths due to thrombosis, and that doctors should therefore pay attention to whether these symptoms occur after vaccination. Efficacy in people with weakened immune systems (i.e., most elderly and chronically ill people): NOT studied.

Effects on pregnant women? NOT known, even the animal studies with this have not been completed. Yet "we do not expect any effects on fetal development. However, pregnant women should only be vaccinated 'if the potential benefit outweighs the potential risks to mother and fetus.' It is also not known whether Vaxzevria passes into breast milk, or if there are any effects on fertility. Again, animal testing has not been completed (but you may WELL serve as a guinea pig).

The Empire claims that the vaccines are "proven and safe," but the manufacturer itself is much less sure, as evidenced by the explanation (pg.7) of the vaccine's genetic encoding of the Spike protein of the SARS-CoV-2 virus, which "may contribute to protection against Covid-19. (bold added) And if the vaccine is accidentally spilled, it should be disinfected with an agent against (adeno)viruses. So: possibly harmful when touched, but not harmful when injected IN your body?

Efficacy and safety in the elderly need not be demonstrated for 3 years

Duration of protection the vaccine would provide? NOT known. Interaction with other medications? NOT studied. Is this really a safe vaccine, and does it really work against Covid-19? Not known until 12 months after vaccination. However, governments did not want to wait for that, and began vaccinating the population shortly after the test phases were concluded.

It is not until May 31, 2022 that the efficacy, stability and safety of this vaccine need to be definitively demonstrated. For the elderly and chronically ill, it will not be until March 31, 2024, or THREE YEARS from now (pg. 16). By then, almost the entire world population will have been vaccinated. Given the above, we might be justified in wondering how many elderly people will have survived these vaccines by then. Because it really does say it, in black and white: only in three years' time does the efficacy and safety of this vaccine need to be definitively demonstrated. (pp.15-16)

Who still dares to claim that this is not an unprecedented mass medical experiment involving the entire world population, the consequences of which, according to a large number of scientists, doctors and other experts, could well be terrible?

What is going on with all these people anyway?

What on earth is the matter with all those gullible people, that they still roll up their sleeves for this? And with all those people who handle the syringes, thus condemning some people to thrombosis, a brain haemorrhage, a chronic (autoimmune) disease or even death?

With the authorities, directors and politicians who commission this, but in the meantime have rejected in advance any liability and responsibility in case things go completely wrong with YOUR health, and perhaps even with your life?

For the answer, I'll just refer briefly to the annals of the 1930s and 1940s again. THAT is what is going on with all these people. They have been seized again by the same dark, mind-numbing and terrorizing spirit of total fear, blindness, absolute obedience and collective mindlessness, which once again seems to be paving the way for unspeakable anti-human crimes with potentially countless numbers of victims.

We have learned NOTHING from history, even recent ones.

Our other books

Check out our other books for other unreported news, exposed facts and debunked truths, and more.

Join the exclusive Rebel Press Media Circle!

You will get a new updates about the unreported reality delivered in your inbox every Friday.

Sign up here today:

https://campsite.bio/rebelpressmedia

9 789494 929163 10